Jokes and More Jokes with Syntax

ISBN 0-533-12626-6

C o n t e n t s

C o n t e n t s

About the Author

Each life is but a book,
Made·up of many a page.
At every chapter that we look,
We complete but just one stage.
In my chapter of comedy,
Laughter is my aim.
So when I face adversities,
A joke eases the pain.
....Something to think about

———————————⬤▬⬤———————————

Why This Book

Laughter releases stress. Jokes provide laughter. When feeling down and life's problems seem insurmountable, it is quite relaxing to have an opportunity to laugh. This booklet aims to satisfy that need.

At events like variety concerts, weddings and comedy shows, where the emcee plays a pivotal role in ensuring that the patrons are entertained, appropriate jokes are crucial. Emcees sometimes worry that people might laugh at them rather than with them. To some persons, worry no more. Just select the jokes suitable for the occasion, fashion them to suit your audience and wait for the congratulations after the show.

In an attempt to keep it clean, many jokes which might be considered unsuitable for the eyes and ears of children were discarded. Some jokes might not come across as funny, but what is ordinary to one person might be viewed as humourous to another.

Those persons relying on this material for reproduction at shows must recognise that one's mannerisms, expressions - facial or otherwise - plus the tone of voice, is important for effective communication of jokes to an audience.

I hope that after reading the material in this booklet, you will find it appealing enough to want to purchase it as a souvenir or as a gift for friends or family.

To those who enjoy my presentation, you must laugh until your belly burst. You must shout out and let the person next door hear.

The Watchman

A young boy from my neighbourhood was very hungry. He decided to break into a house to get something to eat. The telephone rang "Brring, Brring".

The young boy answered the telephone, "Hello, Hello". The person on the line asked who it was.

Hear the boy, "It's the watchman".

"I don't have a watchman", said the owner.

"Well I am sorry" said the boy, "but I am the watchman because I am watching to see when you're coming home".

"I am watching ..."

No Soap

According to the Enquirer of June 3rd,1997, Princess Diana had:

95 gowns

176 dresses

178 suits

54 coats

25 trousers

29 jackets

28 sweaters

71 blouses

14 hats

several ski suits

50 pairs of shoes and boots

more than 200 hand bags and

no soap

was mentioned.

Beer Sport

A man went into a shop to buy a beer. When he asked the shop keeper the cost, he told him two twenty five.

He said twenty-five and twenty-five are fifty cents, so he gave the shop keeper a dollar and asked for his change.

The Refrigerator

An old friend from the district came back home to live. He bought some fish, meat, beer, and drinks, filled up his refrigerator and invited his friends to a party.

Everyone had a good time but there was a friend at the party who felt that if this man could have a party, well he must have one too. He decided that he would take a refrigerator on credit from a leading store. He bought meat like lamb, pork, fish, and chicken as well as plenty drinks. He put them in the 'fridge' and invited his friends to a party too.

On the day of the party when he opened the refrigerator to prepare the meat, he found that the meat was smelling. He could not imagine what was wrong so he called in a refrigerator repair worker.

After checking the plug the repairman found out that the gentleman did not have electricity in the house.

Full Of It

A friend of mine was feeling badly so he decided to weigh himself. He weighed 306 lbs. He went to the doctor who suggested that he should use the toilet. When he came off the bowl he weighed himself again He weighed 205 lbs. He flushed the toilet some 20 times. He was full of it.

Police

People everywhere sometimes get fed up of hearing, the police say that they are **investigating the matter**. When you complain about a burglary, some six months after it happened, the police would say, "We are **investigating the matter**."

You call to tell them that you have seen someone dealing in illegal drugs and you hear; "We are **investigating the matter**."

But if you tell them that a naked woman is running around the district, they will come quickly and apprehend her. When you call to find out if they have everything under control, you hear,"We are **looking into the matter**."

Sweets

In every classroom there is one child who always knows everything. It is always "Please teacher I know.... Please teacher I know."

Well one day the teacher asked, "What is fourteen twos (14 x 2)". Up jumps this chap and said 28.

The teacher was so happy that a child at such a tender age knew the answer, she called him and gave him 28 sweets.

Do you know what the boy went and told his friend?

He said that if he knew that the teacher was giving sweets he would have said ONE HUNDRED.

Operation

Doctors today have me very scared. When you go to them for an amputation they are cutting off the wrong parts.

My grandfather, a diabetic, went to the doctor to have his right leg amputated. After the operation and Grand-dad recovered, he realized that he still had two legs. He couldn't understand.

It was only when he went to pass water that he cried out, "Oh dear, wrong leg!"

Madman

In a mental hospital there are classes in Mathematics. When a patient does well he is usually given the opportunity to go home.

One day a nurse at the hospital decided that it was time for her to test the patients to decide whether they could go home or whether they would stay.

The simple question was "What is 3 times 7?"

The first patient said 84. The nurse said it was not time for him to go.

The next patient said 3 times 7 is Saturday.

Obviously he could not leave either.

The third fellow said 3 times 7 is 21.

He was right so they told him that he could go home.

When he was leaving, the nurse turned to him and asked him how he had arrived at the answer.

He replied, "It was easy mam, I just divided 84 by Saturday."

Madman cont'd...

Just as the nurse was about to prevent him from going home, he asked her to let him explain.

He said Saturday is the seventh (7th) day of the week, and when you divide 84 by 7 the answer is 12. He explained that he was seeing the answer backwards when he said 21.

Complimentary Drinks

I went to a restaurant and bought lunch. I turned to the waitress and asked, "Is the drink complimentary?" She said rather politely, "No, it comes with the meal."

Mosquitoes

This man went into the hospital. At about six o'clock when the sun went down some mosquitoes began to attack him. You should hear him shouting, "Nurse, nurse, nurse!" When the nurse came he would explain that the mosquitoes were attacking him.

The shouts for nurse occurred about four times, so the nurse turned off the lights at about 8 o'clock hoping that this would cause the gentleman to stop calling out to her about the attacks from the mosquitoes.

With the lights off, the gentleman saw some fireflies that were in the room, so he called out to the nurse, "Nurse, nurse, nurse!"

When she came he told her that the mosquitoes were so much out to get him, they brought along lanterns.

First Class

A boy came home boasting that he came first in Mathematics. Asked about his score he said, "I got nine......nine out of one hundred". He went on to say "the other children were absent due to bad weather and the teacher gave him two extra points for braving the weather".

12

Thumpalum

Three sailors were shipwrecked on an Island and were rescued by a group of Arawak Indians. To be set free they had to make a choice between Death and Thumpalum.

The first sailor said that he preferred Thumpalum because he didn't want to die. They took him behind a wall and gave him Thumpalum. He went in walking straight but came out walking with a wring.

The second fellow asked him what was Thumpalum, but all he would say is that he should find out for himself. The second fellow said to give him Thumpalum.

Well he came back hardly able to walk.

This made the third guy afraid. When they asked him whether he wanted Thumpalum or Death, he said that he preferred Death.

Well the Arawaks said, "it's death by Thumpalum."

Two Stones

In England people would never say that they weigh 140 pounds or 210 pounds. You would always hear them say, "I am 10 stones or 15 stones.

Well I know this fat fellow who weighed 30 stones and was dating my friend. She told him that if he were really serious about the relationship he needed to lose 2 stones.

The fellow got castrated.

Rum Punch

A Tourist had four dollars.

A rum punch cost five.

When the tourist came to buy a rum punch,

the barman took the four dollars, poured him four dollars in rum and gave him ONE PUNCH .

Give Off

During a Science lesson a teacher was explaining that plants "breathe" in carbon dioxide and "give off" oxygen, which is then taken in by animals.

The teacher made the mistake and asked the children "what do people give off?" A child in the class said "Stale air Sir."

"What kind of stale air son?" asked the teacher "A FART SIR," replied the boy.

Pussy Cat

A young fellow almost drowned the other day in a water well behind his house.

After taking him out of the water well, his father asked him, "Why did you go into the well?"

The little boy said that his teacher taught him, "Ding Dong Bell. Pussy in the Well", so he went looking.

ZR Blues

My next door neighbour's son was run over by a car. His father called the police. He waited for fifteen minutes, but they did not show up.

He called again and they still did not show up.

He went back into the house, called the police and told them that a ZR (a gypsy cab) was blocking a hydrant. Sirens could be heard in the distance. Twenty three policemen were on the scene in two minutes.

Eleven Portions

In a Chinese restaurant, as you know, there is a menu with different kinds of food being identified with a number.

For example:

The order for number 25 was shrimp, fried rice and vegetables.

The order for number 11 was fried rice, egg and chicken.

An English boy working in this Chinese restaurant got an order for a number 11.

He brought 11 portions of fried rice, egg and chicken.

Breaking and Entering

Adultery is wrong, but some people just can't help. Every morning my brother would go to work leaving his wife to take care of the house.

There was a butcher living in the district, who would watch him. The moment he left home, the butcher would enter the house through the back window. Well! You know what would happen.

A neighbour informed my brother, so one day he turned back. He caught the butcher butchering.

A fight ensued and the police was called. They arrested and charged the butcher with breaking and entering.

In front of the judge he pleaded not guilty. To explain he told the judge that the husband should be the one charged with breaking and entering. He said that while her husband was breaking and entering, he was entering and breaking.

The butcher meant that while entering the bathroom and trying to get out, he broke a glass window.

Long Tail

My son made a kite. He couldn't find a long tail. He called the West Indies cricket team.

Big Boy

Mother and daughter were having a chat. The mother told her daughter that when she gets married, she wanted her to marry a big boy.

She got married to a man (400) four-hundred pounds.

Room-Mate

Advertised in, a local newspaper was "WANTED, ONE ROOM-MATE." The advertiser got someone almost immediately.

The applicant was put in his room and made comfortable. Eight o'clock during the night he left his room, and joined his newly found room-mate in his bed. His room-mate expressed surprise, so the new chap sought to explain.

He told him that he had only given him a ROOM, and that was only part of the deal. He said that he now wanted to MATE.

Millionaire

You can't imagine the things people would do to get rich. A man was caught passing air repeatedly in a crowd of persons. When asked what was his problem.

He said that he wanted to be a million**air**.

Take Note

Imagine buying a new bicycle and on reaching home somebody stealing it. It happened to Robert, so he went and bought another bicycle. The moment he reached home it was stolen again.

Robert decided to buy a video camera, and another bicycle. He set the video camera up so that he could get a shot of the crook who was taking his bicycles.

With the camera running, he left home.

When he returned he found out that the thief had stolen the camera. The thief left a note which read, "Thanks for the camera, had enough bicycles".

Crocodile Tears

A couple was on the brink of separation. The man looked at the lady and told her that he did not love her any more. She started bawling out. She screamed out, "My Lord, I am going to die." She begged somebody to bring her a handkerchief.

The man asked her to stop crying so that he could finish what he was saying. She calmed down, so he continued.

I do not love you any more, nor do I love you any less. She flashed a broad smile.

Not a drop of water in her eyes.

She went and called a friend and told her that if he had called it quits, Harry her boyfriend was there waiting.

One God

During a lesson in Religious Education, a teacher asked. 'How many Gods are there?"

Mary said, fifty. Jackie said one hundred, Tom said one hundred and fifty.

Well, Jack decided that he was not going to wait, because the teacher started beating the children unmercifully.

Just as he eased through the door and crossed the street, Jack met Johnny coming to school late. He told him that the teacher was going mad on the children because they did not know the answer to the question, 'How many Gods are there'?

He warned Johnny not to go to school, but Johnny said that he knew the answer.

When Johnny told Jack that the answer was one God, Jack told him that Jackie had said 100, Mary said 50 and Tom 150. He said, not one of those gods was of any help in preventing them from getting whip.

"Do you expect that one God will be of any help to you?" he asked.

Jack continued, "Well you can go up there with your one God and let the teacher kill you. You see me, I am going home.

The Homeless

Three homeless people, who were tired of sleeping on the side walk, went to the Prime Minister of my country for a job. They wanted money to buy a home.

The Prime Minister asked the first man - an old man who was barely able to walk - what was his name. The old man who was so excited to be speaking with the Prime Minister of the country replied, "Cave Shepherd", because he slept on the pavement outside Cave Shepherd.

The Prime Minister said that he didn't ask him to say where he sleeps. He told him that he only wanted him to give his real name.

The next man said that his name was Fred's Bakery.

He too was cast aside because the Prime Minister thought that he could not answer a simple question.

The third man said that his name was Ken.

The Prime Minister told him to take care of his lawn and he would be paid a decent salary.

Now Friday was pay day, and the accountant wanted the man's complete name, to write it on his cheque. When he asked the man to give his full name he said, "Kentucky Fried Chicken".

20

A Pencil

Some teachers think that they are smarter than the children they teach. One teacher in a lesson requiring the children to use their imagination, put her hand in her pocket and said to the children, "I want you to tell me what is in my hand." She began her description -It is soft, ripe, green and round. Before the teacher had finished a child shouted, "A mango" .

The teacher said, "No, its a pear, but it shows you are thinking".

She went on; hand in pocket again she said, "It is big, white inside with many seeds".

The children shouted, "an English apple".

The teacher said, "No, its a soursop but it shows you are thinking".

A smart boy then said that he wanted to give the teacher one, meaning that he wanted to be the teacher asking the questions, while the teacher gave the answer to his quiz.

He began, "It is long, pointed, hard and has a head with a rubber on top".

The teacher said, "That's enough" in a very vexed manner. The boy then pulled out a pencil from his pocket and showed the teacher.

As the teacher broke into a smile, the child said. "It shows you were thinking.... Dirty"

21

Drunkard

Being drunk and not able to control oneself is a terrible position to be caught in.

A fellow went to a party with this friend. They gave him everything he wanted - from rum to beer to vodka.

Well obviously he got drunk. A group of them took him into a room.

Use your imagination and you know what happened.

When he got up next morning he stretched and said "I like I was 'tight' last night."

A guy lying next to him said. "Only at first."

Elections

During the last elections, a candidate while canvassing, told an old lady that he would repair the road leading to her house. After he won the elections, he apparently did not keep his promise.

While canvassing for the next election, someone told the old lady that the candidate would be visiting her shortly.

The message she gave was, "Tell him for me not to come back in my constitution".

Of course she meant constituency.

Quiz Corner

1. Big Belly Banister baked bad bread. How many B's in that?

2. One is a single
   Two is a double
   Three is a triple
   What is four and five?

3. What is the oldest table?

4. Add ten threes and get seven hundred and five.

5. What's in front of woman that's behind a cow?

6. How can you tell that Santa Claus is a farmer?

7. A frog fell into a well 13 metres deep. Everyday he climbed up five metres but fell back four metres during the night. How many days did he take to get out?

8. How many times is a clock right when it's not working?

9. What happened to the lady who was on a diet and refused to use her tea?

10. The West Indies cricket team was asked to score one hundred and sixty-five runs off two balls. They won the game. How did they do it?

All answers are given on the back page. They are written in ("reverse writing") mirror writing. To obtain the answers place the book in front of a mirror.

Gold

Harold was in love with Rosalind. Everything on her was made of gold. Even her wisdom teeth were covered in gold. The relationship ended when she wanted him to buy her an expensive gold chain for her birthday.

He then met Mary who just loved gold. He soon terminated the friendship when she wanted him to buy a gold bracelet for thousands of dollars.

He vowed never to fall in love with anyone who had anything to do with gold. He met a student. She did not wear gold. This was the woman he wanted.

For her birthday he gave her some money to buy herself a gift. She paid down on a gold chain, then called him and asked for the balance. When he looked at the purchase certificate she had filled out,her middle name was "GOLDENE".

Virgin

A tourist was teaching me some German. He said that in German:

-good morning was good morgan

-good afternoon was good abend

-good day was good intact

He turned to me and asked me if I knew any German. Not wanting to embarrass myself I said "Yes". He then asked me what was the German for virgin.

I said "good and tight".

24

Plants

In a science lesson the children were asked to show a real plant which was to be collected from outside the classroom during the lunch break.

Going around the class to inspect each plant, the teacher came upon Joe, who started trembling and crying because he did not have a plant.

Joe began to unzip his pants. The teacher asked him why he was unzipping his pants. He explained that he did not have a plant, but he had two seeds. He told her that he was thinking, she could plant them.

Application Form

NAME	:	TIM but they call me Timothy for short.
A DRESS	:	Wear pants only.
SEX	:	Never had.
SPOUSE	:	Mrs. Palmers nicknamed "Five Fingers"
AGE	:	Eight and three quarter years.
D. O. B.	:	February 29 once in a while
INTEREST	:	5% at the Bank.

Anxious

There was a little boy who was eager to go to school but was too small to do so.

When it was time to go because he had reached school age, he smiled and got ready about three hours before school began.

Next morning, when his mother woke him to get ready for school he began quarrelling. He said, "but Mummy, Mummy, didn't I go yesterday?"

Grandfather's Death

One of the rules of the school I attended was that when you were absent, you should bring a letter explaining the reason for your absence.

There was a boy named Charles who lived with his grandfather. Charles did not attend school one Monday, and when he came the following day he started to explain to the teacher that his grandfather had died.

The teacher turned to him and asked, "But where is your letter?"

He said that his grandfather did not give him any.

The teacher insisted he show a letter.

He said in that case, take me to the undertaker.

The Poker Game

An American, a Trinidadian and a Barbadian decided to play a game of poker. Before the game began it was decided that each person would start the game with five dollars. The American put five American dollars on the table. The Barbadian then put down five Barbados dollars. The Trinidadian then put down twenty ("TT") Trinidadian dollars. He took up the five American dollars and five Barbados dollars and demanded his five dollar change.

N.B. Twenty Trinidadian dollars ($20.00) is worth approximately three American dollars ($3.00).

Favourite Colour

An artist met this attractive lady and fell in love with her immediately. It was love at first sight. He proposed to her.

She told him that she would marry him if he could tell her the name of her favourite colour. He began calling the names of different colours. Some of them unheard of. When he couldn't come up with the correct one he did some research and started again, Amber, magenta, cyan...

He finally gave up and asked what was her favourite colour.

Can you imagine she told him, she did not have a favourite colour.

Would you believe that:

1. My mother is so bad at growing plants that even artificial ones die on her.

2. A two year old child was asked how old he was. He said too old.

3. A man travelling on a single engine plane without a toilet, asked the pilot to park so that he could pass water.

4. When a girl told her brother he was on television, he turned it on only to find the programme, 'Monkeys and Chimpanzees.'

5. Beulah wore a dress filled with holes to church because the preacher told her she was holy.

6. A man who loved big women got his girlfriend pregnant whenever she got small.

7. A boy's sister wrote the sentence: 'The boy's pen is in my hand', on the computer. He went and removed the space between the 'pen' and 'is'. The sister kept reading it over and over.

8. A lady asked me for a description of myself. I told her to look for a very handsome guy. When she entered the party, she came straight to me and asked me if I were Bing Bong.

9. A fire-station was built near an airport to handle any crash that might occur. The first aeroplane to crash, crashed into the fire-station.

10. A man who was married for 25 years was asked if he had any children. He said no. Before he could explain his wife said that up until today he didn't get any yet.

Man Hole

As I was driving to town one day, I saw Harold standing next to a sign which read OPEN MAN HOLE. When I passed back two hours later he was still standing there. I decided to find out what was his problem.

He pointed out that the sign says 'OPEN MAN HOLE'. He told me he was waiting there because he didn't have _EX for a long time.

Job

Some people want a job but they don't want to work. A hotel worker applied for a job which was advertised in the local newspaper. In his contract he negotiated for three weeks vacation and a daily lunch hour.

When he was given the O.K. to start work, he asked if he could start with his vacation.

Prisioner

A convicted prisoner was placed in front of a firing squad, but the squad was placed on hold because they were awaiting word from the governor as to whether or not the governor would pardon the convict.

A few minutes before word came from the governor, an ant crawled up the man's leg and bite him. The prisoner shouted "Oh shoot".

Watching A Seat

While at the airport, I overheard a lady sitting next to me asking a gentleman to watch her seat. She wanted to go to the washroom.

When she got up, this fellow started walking around behind her.

Wicket Keeper

In the game of Cricket, the wicket keeper is the person behind the three sticks called stumps or wicket. Without the wicket the game cannot be played.

When the school's cricket team was picked, the captain asked Andrew if he would be the wicket keeper and 'keep wicket'.

The next day when the match was to begin, the players couldn't find the stumps.

The wicket keeper kept the wicket (stumps) at home.

Swimsuits

There was this lady who had twenty-three bathing suits. She had a habit of sleeping in them.

Her cousin saw the swimsuits in her wardrobe, and remarked that he didn't see the point of her having so many swimsuits when they don't get wet.

She remarked, "You'll be surprised."

F•A•R•T

Fat Albert Riccardo Thomas died when his car ran off the road and struck a pole. At the autopsy the local doctors could not find out the cause of death. Specialists from overseas brought in a Fowl Air Recording Tester otherwise known as a **Fart-ometer**. When they had finished their test they concluded that he died because he passed air in the car with windows rolled up.

It was the **F•A•R•T** (First Accident Recorded There).

May Not

Mark who was getting married was uncertain about whether he wanted to continue with the wedding.

Instead of calling it off, he sent out the invitations with the date of the wedding being May 0. (naught)

Asked about it he said that he May not bother.

Bill

A woman saw a man going into a ladies washroom and shouted; "Hey skipper, you are going into the wrong washroom".

The man looked around at her and said; "Wait Miss Lady, do you want to tell me who I am?

Avoid Fat

A gentleman who was experiencing problems with his liver went to his doctor.

The doctor told him that he must avoid fat where possible.

The man stopped sleeping next to his wife.

Early Tom

A school boy who was always late for school was seen at school on a Monday bank holiday when school was closed.

The teacher who was passing by stopped and asked him if he didn't remember that school was closed.

He said, "You see sir, you are always complaining that I am always late, so I decided to be early for Tuesday.

A Slice

While at Teacher Training College a student asked the cook serving meals for another slice of potato because she only had one slice on her plate. When she reached out with her plate expecting another slice, Mrs. Wickham, the cook cut the piece of potato on her plate in two.

Flossy

Flossy was a pet dog, who was liked by his owner very much. Flossy's favourite spot was in the living room.

When visitors came by, Flossy would always lay near the visitors' feet as if listening to the conversation.

One day this friend visited and would you believe the friend seemed to have had a problem with air. He just kept passing air all the time.

Every five minutes he would ease up his leg and pass air, when he saw that his host was not looking.

Every time the foul air was smelt the host would say to Flossy, "Outside Flossy, Outside!" as if to blame the dog.

On the fourth occasion, Flossy turned his face. The dog's owner, who cared for the dog, grabbed hold of the dog and said, "Don't you stand there and let this man poison you". With that he took Flossy outside.

At the Restaurant

At a leading restaurant a sign read, "Welcome, PLEASE WAIT TO BE SEATED". A waiter passed and accidentally knocked off the 'S' from the word seated. It then read, 'Welcome, PLEASE WAIT TO BE EATED'.

Would you believe that a gentleman came to lunch with his wife and she started undressing.

Love

A school boy in an attempt to impress a girl in his class looked at her and said, "When I look into your eyes I see love. I see the magnet in them that wants to pull me towards you".

The girl smiled. He asked her, "What do you see in mine?"

She looked and said that the only thing she saw was "cold".

(In Barbados "Cold" is "Yampee", the mucous that develops in the corner of the eye.)

Toilet Paper

A boy went to the store to buy some rabbit food.

The store owner said to him that if he needed rabbit food he should bring the rabbit.

The next day the boy said he wanted to buy some dog chow. The owner said, "listen youngster if you had to bring that cat yesterday won't you expect that I would want you to bring the dog today". The boy turned away and went back home.

Two hours later the boy returned with a brown paper bag. He told the store owner to put his hand inside the bag.

When he did, he pulled it out and said "yuk, that's dirty".

The boy said, well give me two rolls of toilet paper.

34

Life

Authorities here are extremely harsh with drug offenders. A prisoner who was spending life behind bars was caught with drugs. He was sentenced to spend two more years in prison.

Aids

Joe went out with Harriet. It was the first time after meeting her on the bus.

Neither could exercise self-control so they got down to business.

At the end of the exercise Joe thought he would play a prank on Harriet, so he said to her, "But you know sweetheart, I have AIDS".

"What!" she exclaimed. Then in a soft tone she said, "No problem, I have it too".

For Sale

While in Brooklyn on holiday, my father had put a refrigerator out on the pavement to be collected. The refrigerator stayed there for two days. The garbage truck kept passing it.

My father, annoyed because it was not collected, took the refrigerator back inside.

One day an idea struck him. He took the refrigerator back outside but this time put **'FOR SALE'** on it. He oniy went back inside to put down the marker and when he looked outside the refrigerator was gone.

Perspiration

A Bajan met this lady and thought that she was the prettiest one he had ever met. He asked her out to a dance but he was not impressed with the way she smelt.

On his way to the dance, he kept his nose through the window.

After reaching the dance hall and actually dancing, the smell got worse, so he asked her what kind of deodorant she uses.

Her reply was, "The only deodorant I use is perspiration."

She turned and asked him if he liked it. Would you believe he had the "gall" to say YES.

Bicycle

A body-builder went riding one morning and forgot that he had to go to work. When he realized it, he was some twelve miles away from home. Luckily, he saw this friend in a Toyota sports car who lived in his district, so he stopped him and explained.

The driver went to the back of the car, tied a piece of rope from the car onto the bicycle and instructed the rider that if he should go too fast for him all he needed to do was ring the bell and he would slow down.

Well, they got started.

Five minutes later, the driver of the Toyota saw a fellow in a sports car that he had always wanted to race. He took up the challenge forgetting the rider. He came within two car lengths of the other car when a guy standing outside his house saw what was happening. He ran inside quickly and reported it to his mother.

He said, "Mother I just saw two sports cars racing down the road and the car in front had only two lengths on the second one. They were travelling at over 100 m.p.h. That is true mummy", he said, "and you know what I saw? I saw a man with a bicycle behind the car ringing his bell, trying to pass.

Ugliness

Two men were arguing about who had the ugliest wife. The argument was so intense that they decided to prove it to each other. They cast a bet of $200.00. The person with the ugliest wife would win.

The first fellow told the other that if he went up the beach, he would see his wife at the present moment frightening Sea Gulls.

The fellow set off right away. He returned and said that the first man's wife was not really ugly.

The second man then invited him to go to his home and check out his wife. They left right away.

On his way home the second guy told the other man he would lose his money, but guaranteed him that he would get one million dollars worth of ugliness. When they got home, the man called out to his wife, "Honey I have someone here eager to meet you.

"To meet me?" she asked.

"Yes", he replied.

She said, "Okay, hold on and let me put a pillow case over my face."

He shouted back to her that it was not necessary, as he was not ready to make love.

She came upstairs and the visiting fellow just burst out laughing. The gentleman just told the visitor to give him the $200.00.

Getting Hard

When refrigerators first came into being, Mark realised that when he put water into the refrigerator it became hard. He also realised that when he put hotdogs into the freezer they became hard.

One day Mark's wife came home saying that she felt like making love. Mark jumped into the freezer.

Cockroach

A teacher who was teaching compound words made this sentence. The cockroach ran up the wall.

He explained that the word cockroach was made up of two words cock and roach. He then turned to a student and asked him to make a sentence with roach, leaving out the word cock.

The student said, "The roach ran up the wall with cock out".

Time or Thyme

Robert was broke. He needed money quickly. He went to his garden and harvested some thyme. He took it to the village shopkeeper who usually buys it cash.

When he gave it to her she told him that he'll have to give her time.

Have you Heard?

Have you heard of the lady who lived alone but put a towel around her after bathing because the newscaster on television was looking at her?

———————●══●———————

Have you heard of the movie Fidel Castro was making when so many Cuban boat-people were fleeing Cuba? It was "HOME ALONE."

———————●══●———————

Have you heard of the teacher who could not find where his student lived?

Teacher: Where do you live?

Student: At my mother.

Teacher: Where does your mother live?

Student: Above Ms. Browne's shop.

Teacher: Where is Ms Browne's shop?

Student: Well it would have to be below my mother's house.

Teacher: Can you give me directions to your house?

Student: Well, come up the road, turn so and then so (pointing with the hand) and you will see a bridge. Ask the boys on the bridge.

———————●══●———————

Have you heard of the famous case of Lorenza Bobbit? She said that her husband lost the case, because after she had cut it off, the evidence didn't, couldn't and wouldn't stand up in court.

Have you heard of the bishop who was interviewed by a group of nuns. They asked him, what kind of meat he likes. He said nun.

Have you heard of this couple?

- The wife couldn't see eye to eye with her husband because he was blind.
- She could not reach down to his level because he was too short.
- She made him feel real down.

Have you heard of the blind man who asked a cashier to change a hundred dollar note? The lady gave him four twenties and a five. He said, "this don't look right".

Have you heard of the man who went to the doctor and when the doctor said "Blow" he shouted, "Pram-pram" just like a car.

When the doctor said, "Not so", the man said "Keek-keek" just like a van.

The doctor, realising that he didn't understand asked him to stop. He said "Eeerrks", a screeching sound as if he had applied brakes.

Have you heard of the girl who was making love to her partner and asked him if he had protection?

Would you believe it? He pulled out a gun and said that he was not afraid of anybody.

Have you heard of the boy in the class who, when asked what was 99 threes said - a forest.

Organ

Don't you ever do like me. I went to learn how to play the mouth organ. When the instructor told me to take out my organ you wouldn't believe what I took out. A Chinese next to me took out a tiny tiny organ.

Bad Habit

Too much rum is bad. After drinking with friends this alcoholic would come home every night and out of habit he would spit through the window and jump in the bed.

Every single night he would spit through the window and jump in the bed.

One night he came home drunk, spit in the bed and jump through the window.

He broke the habit and the window

Just Made It

People in Manhattan, have great difficulty finding somewhere to urinate, when shopping in that city.

A visitor wanted to pass water. He almost wet himself when he remembered that there were toilets in the Port Authority building. He rushed in, took it out, and in a hurry he began to pass water.

He looked over to the guy standing next to him and said, "Just made it!!, just made it!!".

The guy looked across, open his eyes wide, wide, wide. He asked him, "Can you make one for me too".

Afar

Looking at this lady from some distance, a guy said she is good looking from 'far.

When he got closer he realised she was far from good looking when near.

The Concert

Had this concert in the Bronx. It was twenty dollars to enter. Everyone was standing on the outside and refused to go in.

The organiser of the concert realising no one intended to go in, invited everyone to enter without paying.

When the concert was over he told them they had to pay twenty dollars to get out.

Period

A teacher was late for school because she missed her regular bus. She therefore could not teach her first lesson.

The teacher went to the principal to explain the reason for her not teaching the first lesson.

She said, "Sir, I missed my period".

Before she could say more, the principal said, "My dear you must be pregnant."

N.B.: To miss a teaching session is to miss a period.

43

Chicken Pox

Little children can be such darlings. One evening a little boy's skin began itching him. He went to his mother who told him, he was probably catching chicken pox because she saw some small bumps on his skin. The little boy turned to her and said that he can remember eating chicken but he didn't eat any pox.

Condoms

A boy's mother asked him to buy some balloons to decorate the house for Christmas. He bought a box of condoms. He told his mother that they were at bargain price, three for the price of one.

Marriage

My very good friend was getting married so he sent off the invitation some six weeks prior to the wedding. About a week before the wedding he wanted to call it off. He tried to persuade his fiance to call it off but she wouldn't.

A day before the wedding an idea struck him. He burned down the church.

Ugly Teacher

A teacher in a spelling lesson called on a child to spell passenger. He spelt it correctly.

Another child was asked to spell temperature. He also spelt it correctly.

When the teacher called on the third boy to spell ugliness the boy said, "Y.O.U".

Cutting Trees

A friend of mine had some trees to cut down. They were difficult to cut and no one wanted to help cut them. Up came this fellow from Guyana and in three days the trees were cut down. It was unbelievable.

Hearing of this man, a Trinidadian manufacturer, who wanted some material to build chairs, sent for him in Guyana to cut down what seemed like a forest.

The manufacturer said to the fellow that at his speed he should take six months to cut down the trees. In one month the trees were cut down.

A woman who saw the man cutting down the trees, asked him, where he learned to cut trees.

He said "In the Sahara."

She exclaimed, "The Sahara! The Sahara is a desert and don't have trees."

He said, "Do you expect the Sahara to have trees when I cut down all of them?"

Poor Granny

I thought that my granny was smart. This was until she bought some mangoes, one hundred mangoes for one hundred dollars.

She sold them at five for four dollars and complained to me that she was not making any profit.

Liar

A student at the university did not do an assignment.

Her tutor asked her for it , and she told him that she had done the assignment but had forgotten to print it off the computer.

The tutor offered to take her home. When he got to the house, she did not have a computer.

Lovemones

A woman injected her dog with a hormone. This allowed her dog to detect when a man was seriously in love with her or was just lusting.

When a person was lusting the dog gave of LUSTMONES.

When he was seriously in love LOVEMONES were given off.

One Thursday a guy called up for a date. She got her dog ready.

A long walk, a chat and LOVEMONES were flowing. When they reached home he refused to get close to her. She couldn't understand.

When she asked, "why?"

He said that he was in love with the dog

Waitress

A waitress at a leading hotel informed me that she could save me some money, if she purchased my lunch at staff rate. If I bought it, the lunch would cost $13.00. I inquired of her what was the staff rate. She said $12.99

Lady with the Lamp

A worker from the electric company went to a lady's house to read the meter. After reading it for six consecutive months, he realized that every month the bill never reached more than three dollars ($3.00).

Out of curiosity the 'meter maid' asked the lady what she does to keep her bill so low, since the others in the neighbourhood pay more that sixty dollars ($60.00) a month.

The old lady said in her squeaky voice, "You see son, all I does do is turn on the electricity to see how to light me lamp."

Current

Did you hear of the man who after the electricity went off took his television set to the sea so as to watch his favourite picture?

He said that he was getting current from the sea. He also told his wife that while he was there he would collect some soap powder too, as his clothes wanted washing.

"What soap powder?", she asked.

"Tide", he replied,. "There's always tide there - high tide or low tide".

She told him to bring her some "Breeze" also, since the wind was blowing strong.

NB: Like Tide, Breeze is the name of a local soap powder.

47

Calves

I was at the stadium when some cyclists were preparing for a race. The riders had some huge feet with some very big calves. Everyone admired their physique.

Surprisingly the last cyclist walked through the gate and on to the field pulling two cows with one hand and carrying his bicycle in the other.

When questioned about it. He said that his calves were not big enough so he brought along two cows.

True Friends

A good friend of the family invited me to his house a Saturday morning. He said that he had invited about twenty other men because he wanted them to help him with a pressing matter.

Some of his friends refused to go to cricket and football. Others decided to stay at home and did not go to work. I did not go to church because I considered him a good friend of the family.

When everyone arrived at his house, and asked him what he wanted done.

He said he wanted us to help him catch a mouse.

Disappointed

A lady from my neighbourhood told me that she was going overseas to be married. She said that she had fallen in love with a tourist who was vacationing here.

My neighbour said that her husband to be loves her and her son. He told her that he would treat her well.

She left one Thursday and called me the next day to tell me that she was coming back.

When I asked what is the problem.

She said that he turned out to be a she.

A Number

A little boy went to his teacher and told her that he wanted to urinate. The teacher told him that the next time he wanted to pass water, he must say that he wants to No.1.

A few minutes later another pupil said that she wanted to "stool". The teacher told the little girl that the next time she wanted to "stool" she must say that she wants to No. 2.

While she was explaining that to the little girl, a little boy shouted; "Please teacher, Please Teacher!", give me a number quick, I want to pass air.

For a different experience the congregation of the Small Time Revival Hall decided to go an Anglican Church for their Sunday worship. The group was small so they did not give advance notice of their intention to the rector of the Holy Day Anglican Church.

The church was almost empty when they arrived. The priest smiled. He felt he was blessed with such a gathering. This was the first time that he would have more than ten persons attending the service. This was his morning to preach the word of God.

He welcomed all and soon began singing a well known hymn. All joined in. What a time they were having. Before the hymn was finished Suzietoofast started singing a number from her church. It was a chorus well known by her flock. Cymbals started coming out of bags. A lady who had two "tots" strapped to her dress began beating them in rhythm and time. Others from the Small Time Revival Hall started beating the benches. It was pandemonium.

The priest started shouting "Silence, Silence!!" They hardly noticed him. Every time he said silence, he was greeted with the repetitive words of Halleluiah, Halleluiah" or "Amen, Amen".

Suzietoofast started pointing her index finger at the regular members of the Anglican church, shouting "Sickiemassiah. Sickiemassiah". This made those members get up and sing.

The whole church was soon dancing. They were praying, they were kneeling and talking in what seemed to be tongues. It was clear that Suzietoofast was their appointed leader. She walked around touching her new found flock on their heads, offering a prayer of some sort.

No one recognized that the priest had made his exit, to the church's annex a stone throw away. He had gone to call the police.

With words of "Quiet please, quiet please and silence!!" he re-entered what was now a Small Time Revival Hall assembly. Suzietoofast pointed her finger at him, and with word Sickiemassiah he started to dance. No one believed a priest could dance like that. The song they were sing was 'Bring them in to Lord Jesus'. People stopped their cars to observe. All it took was a point of the finger from Suzietoofast and the word Sickiemassiah. They started pouring in, a nurse, an artist, a truck driver, a mason, a carpenter, a bus full of tourists, two cricketers who were to open the batting at the village playing field, a gardener and many more filed in when the congregation leader cast her spell.

Sirens could be heard in the distance, they got louder by the minute. Suzietoofast positioned herself at the door. Out jumped two officers. With clubs in hand. They started coming. Suzie just pointed her finger. Clubs turned to percussion instruments. Police started dancing, gyrating to the rhythm.

Hours passed, the crowd got bigger and bigger. Songs were sung over and over. No one got hungry. The priest sat in a pew to take a rest. He fell off to sleep. Suzietoofast then led the congregation to the pasture some distance away.

Only the priest remained. Finally he had silence.

One evening, tired and hungry after a long day at the office, I jumped into my mean machine and started out on what I thought would be my regular journey home. Outside was cold, the wind was blowing in sudden gusts, and it was beginning to look dark and gloomy.

With one turn of the engine I was rolling. Up the road and around the bend I went. Traffic for some unknown reason was backed up. I waited for about half an hour and there was no movement.

Suddenly an idea struck me. Why not turn off through a side street and find my way around the traffic. To do so I thought would be dangerous. I had heard many stories of people being attacked and robbed in the district adjacent to the street. There was talk of dogs and mosquitoes attacking strangers. However, I decided to take a chance.

With one turn of the handle and a bark of the engine, I started out on an escapade which is forever etched in the hallway of my mind.

I turned right, then left, only to find that I had reached a cul -de- sac. With no where to turn, I looked over my shoulder to reverse. Standing behind me was a dog as huge as a horse, barking as loud as a cow would moo. His body was positioned half way across the street

I rolled up my window, I put out my cigarette which I had lit to ease the tension of the afternoon. With one wheel on the kerb, I eased past what had looked like a monster to me. I made a turn in the driveway of an abandoned house. With a screeching sound of smoking tires, I was off again.

Two sharp rights led me into a very depressed area. Signs were hanging from electric poles. The few which were standing were pointing in the wrong direction. It was clear that government workers were too afraid to venture into this district, so the men folk were probably the ones who tacked them up out of position.

The road turned into craters. The stench of garbage filled the air. Windows were either coming off or were off completely. Makeshift doors were of hardboard panels.

I began to feel depress. Could poverty and squalour really be of such magnitude? Children bathing in their birth-suits at the standpipe; two men pulling at a pretty lass making her way to that same standpipe for her bucket of water. Froth coming from the mouth of a few men folk who sat in the rum shop 'firing one', made me feel sad.

Suddenly my engine went silent. For some reason it conked out on me. Sweat soon started pouring down my cheek. "What should I do?" was the question I asked myself. "Get out, run or should I sit patiently and wait until the police pass". These were some of the ideas running through my head. Mosquitoes had begun to come out, dogs were on both sides of the street. Should I just scream!

I did. I woke up. My scream turned to a smile.

Do You Know Any Jokes?
Write Them Here

Syntax

What is Syntax?

1. Syntax is not a crossword despite some similarities.

2. In Syntax diamonds are used. The letters which spell the words are placed in them.

3. All words to be placed in the diamonds provided are taken from the passage which tells the related joke.

4. Clues given do not always give a definition of a word. They are clues to help you find the correct word.

5. There are two variations of Syntax.

   Syntax I: Finding the jumbled word

   Syntax II :   The link up

Words will now be selected from the above sentences to create the two variations of Syntax.

Examples are given on the next two pages

Syntax I

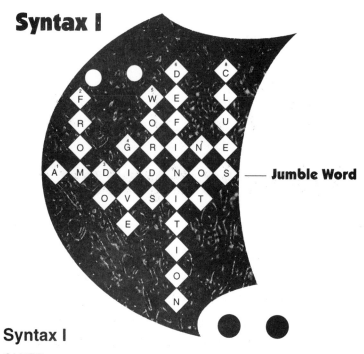

—— **Jumble Word**

Syntax I

CLUES

1. Indefinite article
2. Point of starting
3. When you act
4. Offer
5. Made from letters
6. A description of something
7. Homonym for knot
8. Pointers

Parts of Speech

4. Verb
5. Noun
6. Noun
7. Adverb
8. Noun

The Jumble Word is 'Diamonds'

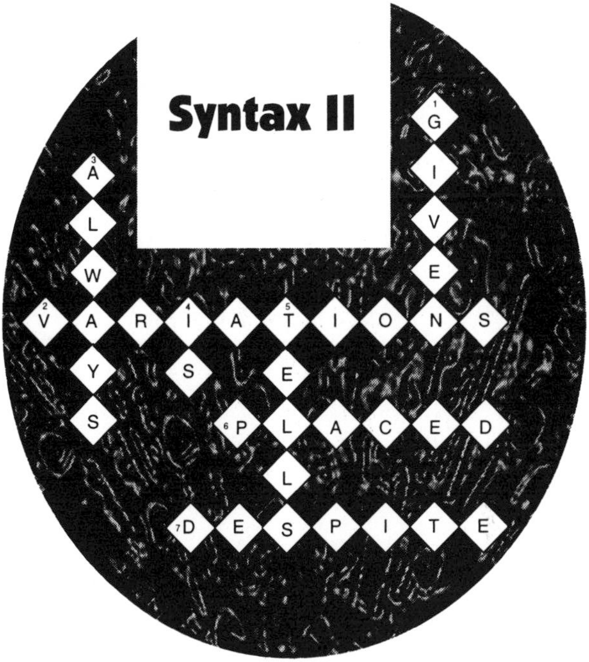
Syntax II
G
I
V
E
N
A
L
W
A
Y
S
V
A
R
I
A
T
I
O
N
S
S
E
P
L
A
C
E
D
L
D
E
S
P
I
T
E

Syntax II

ACROSS

2. Different approaches
6. Put into a position
7. Regardless

Parts of Speech

2. ____________________

6 ____________________

7. ____________________

DOWN

1. Already passed on
3. Forever
4. Sometimes a helping verb
5. To make a report

Parts of Speech

1. ____________________

3. ____________________

4. ____________________

5. ____________________

Deaf and Dumb

While in Miami on my way home, up came this lady. She was one of the prettiest I had ever seen. She gave me a card which read, I AM DEAF AND DUMB. PLEASE GIVE ME TWO DOLLARS TO HELP ME EARN A LIVING.

Quite suspicious of her demeanour. I looked up and said to her, "You know something, if you only tell me that you love me I would give you twenty dollars".

She looked at me, smiled and said, "Do you think that I am foolish?"

Monkey

Some Bajan monkeys were constantly picking mangoes from this farmer's tree. He decided to hire some folks to catch the monkeys.

Well Jack, who was one of the ugliest men in the district decided that since nobody would employ him, he would have a go at catching these monkeys.

There was a time when Jack got a job and when he went to work everyone ran out. When Jack put on a mask, instead of being ugly he was good looking.

Anyway, he decided to catch these monkeys. Up and down the hills he ran after the monkeys. At one stage Jack came up close behind a monkey. The monkey looked back and asked, 'Wait Jack, are they chasing you too?"

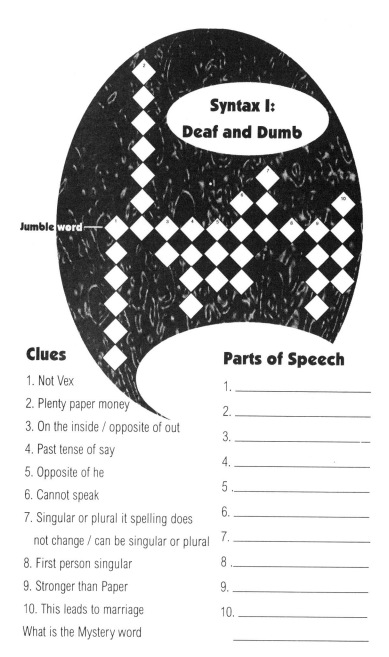

Syntax I: Deaf and Dumb

Jumble word ——

Clues

1. Not Vex
2. Plenty paper money
3. On the inside / opposite of out
4. Past tense of say
5. Opposite of he
6. Cannot speak
7. Singular or plural it spelling does not change / can be singular or plural
8. First person singular
9. Stronger than Paper
10. This leads to marriage

What is the Mystery word

Parts of Speech

1. _____
2. _____
3. _____
4. _____
5. _____
6. _____
7. _____
8. _____
9. _____
10. _____

_____

The Artist

A teacher asked his students to draw a picture of a bone. Well this boy who could draw really well, drew a bone. It looked so real, a dog ate it.

To explain what happened to the teacher the boy drew a picture of the dog.

When the boy gave the picture to the teacher, the teacher accidentally puts his hands in the dog's mouth. The dog bite him.

The teacher could not believe that the boy could draw so well , so he told him to draw another dog in front of him. When the boy finished the drawing, the two dogs began to fight.

The teacher had to throw water on them to separate them.

Smoking

In some countries smoking is prohibited on public buses. In Baruba, smoking is allowed in the two rear seats of the bus.

One night a chain smoker with a lit cigarette boarded a bus and instead of sitting at the rear he went and sat next to the driver.

The driver got angry and asked him if he didn't see that smoking was allowed only in the two rear seats.

The smoker said, "Sorry! I thought the bus was going in the opposite direction".

Syntax II: Artist

Across

2. Complete
4. Pupils
6. Instructor
7. Genuine
8. Caught at a tap or faucet
9. Past tense of draw
10. Loved by a dog

Down

1. Diagram
3. Kept apart
5. Toss

Parts of Speech

2. _____
4. _____
6. _____
7. _____
8. _____
9. _____
10. _____

Parts of Speech

1. _____
3. _____
5. _____

Dollars

An American who went on vacation in Guyana was arrested for stealing one hundred dollars. A decision had to be made as to whether they should try him in Guyana or in the United States.

The defendant decided that he would prefer to have the case heard in the United States.

When they took him back there, he got off because after converting the currency, the judge realized that the man had stolen nothing.

Positive

A friend of mine went to the doctor to have an AIDS test, because his former girlfriend had died of AIDS.

He left the office and kept thinking about whether or not he had contracted the disease. The moment he got home he called the doctor to ask for the results. Obviously the results were not ready.

The doctor told him, "Don't worry, Think POSITIVE."

Rapist

A rapist was in a district terrifying the women folk. In fact he had raped three women and everyone was making sure that the windows and doors were properly secured.

In the district lived this faggot. He put on a lady's dress and left his door wide open.

Syntax II: Positive

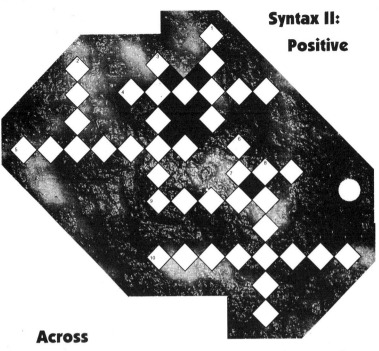

Across

4. Same as previous
5. The end products
7. To question
9. All set
10. Not negative

Down

1. People living together
2. Dreaded disease
3. Takes care of the sick
6. Past tense of have
8. Arrange of words in a sentence

Parts of Speech

4. _____
5. _____
7. _____
9. _____
10._____

Parts of Speech

1. _____
2. _____
3. _____
6. _____
8. _____

Lotto

Dick a sexton spent most of his money buying Lotto tickets. He was in his bed dreaming of winning the Lotto when a fairy godmother appeared. She told him that she would grant him a single wish.

Dick was so excited he wished that whatever he had would become ten times bigger.

His wife couldn't get through the door.

She said that she was not vex because he Dick would now be able to satisfy her.

A Light

A smoker asked his partner for a light. He gave him a searchlight.

Getting Children

A plantation manager tried for many years to get children from his wife. He couldn't get any.

One day he met a worker who said that he was an expert on getting children. The manager paid him a sum of money for him to tell the secret.

He said that both should start by bathing together, then kissing is important. He said, "squeeze her tightly, and when she is ready call him".

Syntax II: Lotto

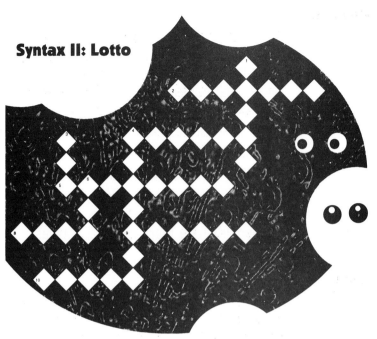

Across

2. To go between

5. Everything

8. At entrance of house

9. Take care of Church property

10. Imaginary being, with magical powers

Parts of Speech

2. _____

5. _____

8. _____

9. _____

10. _____

Down

1. Used to purchase goods

3. At present

4. Content

6. Opposite of him

7. Not please

Parts of Speech

1. _____

3. _____

4. _____

6. _____

7. _____

Miscount

A child at a summer camp was asked to count from one to one hundred. He began one, two, three, four, five, six, seven, eight, nine, ten and so on until he reached twenty-five. When he reached twenty-five he started counting from one again.

The teacher stopped him at five and asked him why he stopped and began again.

He said that he figured that four twenty-fives were equal to one hundred, so he was going to count from one to twenty-five four times.

Nation

In Barbados one of the leading newspapers is called the Nation. It reports on the buying of golf courses, the privitisation of beaches and so on.

A tourist came up to this newspaper vendor and asked him, "How much is it to buy a Nation?"

The vendor told him ten dollars ($10.00) per square foot.

Next Teller Please

My son has to be the smartest boy in the world. One day we went into the bank and there on the counter was the sign, NEXT TELLER PLEASE. He looked across at the next teller and said to me, "Daddy she don't look please; she look vex".

Syntax II: Miscount

Across

2. Half dozen

3. Single

4. Two fours (2x4)

6. The lives of a cat

Parts of Speech

2. _____

3. _____

4. _____

6. _____

Down

1. Homonym for too

2. Number before eight

5. These years make a decade

Parts of Speech

1. _____

2. _____

5. _____

Cane

In the West Indies where the sugar cane is grown, it is often difficult to get people to harvest the cane.

One day, a very poor young lady was asked why she did not go into the fields to cut canes, so as to get some money to feed her two starving children.

She said, "You aint see what Cain did to Abel? Well!! I making sure Cane don't do it to me too"

A Letter

Imagine a man who had no one to love him, boasting that he had received a love letter. He showed it to me and it read:-

You are the sunlight of my rainy days.

You are the seed in my mango when the flesh is gone.

You are my appetite when I don't want to eat.

Then when I reached the end of the letter, by mistake he had signed it to himself from himself.

68

Syntax I: Cane

Jumble word —

Clues

1. Reaped
2. Past tense of do
3. An object of neuter gender
4. Woman with good qualities
5. To give food
6. Homonym for cane
7. Opposite of his
8. Act of creating

What is the jumble word

Parts of Speech

1. _____
2. _____
3. _____
4. _____
5. _____
6. _____
7. _____
8. _____

_____

Loaves

There was an eating competition with all kinds of food to be eaten. The first person to finish his portion would win a new car. The foods to be eaten were: 4 bowls of soup, 2 pig-heads, 8 chicken legs and 12 loaves of bread.

The man who almost won, was a man who had eaten the bowls of soup, the pig heads, chicken legs and eleven of the loaves.

When he got to the last loaf, he could not get it into his mouth. He tried and tried until he managed to get half of it into his mouth. When he realized that the other half would not go down he said that if he had known that the last loaf would have given him so much trouble, he would have eaten that one first.

Too Short

Can you imagine a man being too short to step up on the side-walk?

Bank Robbery

A fellow robbed a bank. The cashier could not believe it when the robber refused to take the dollar notes. In fact he kept insisting that he wanted **cents** only.

When he was apprehended by the police his story was "My girlfriend told me that I did not have any **sense**, so I wanted to get some".

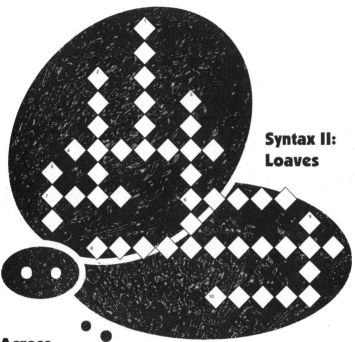

Syntax II: Loaves

Across

4. Amount
6. Soup containers
7. To go in
9. One against another
10. Opposite of taken

Parts of Speech

4. _____
6. _____
7. _____
9. _____
10. _____

Down

1. Primary
2. Nearly
3. A problem
5. Opposite of her
8. Beneath or below

Parts of Speech

1. _____
2. _____
3. _____
5. _____
8. _____

Syntax II: Getting Babies

Across

3. Small Children

5. All

7. Not the full amount

8. Large green fruit

10. Use it to see

Parts of Speech

3. _____

5. _____

7. _____

8. _____

10. _____

Down

1. When you don't forget

2. Often mistaken for a pronoun

4. At the rear

6. Extremely

9. A snake-like fish

Parts of Speech

1. _____

2. _____

4. _____

6. _____

9. _____

Getting Babies

You know how we like to tell lies about where babies come from. I remember when I was very young my mother said that my sister came from in a breadfruit tree. Every breadfruit tree I saw since then I would just look up in it, looking for another sister.

It so happened that when my son asked me where babies come from this is what I told him.

"Well son, all you need is a small bottle, pass some water in it, put it behind the toilet bowl and by the next morning the baby is there."

He did just what I told him. The next morning he went and checked. Inside the bottle was a one eye tadpole. He swore it was an eel. He sucked his teeth real long at the baby frog and said, "Now don't tell anyone that I am your father".

"Now don't tell anyone..."

Dog Bone

Imagine two couples - one from America and the other from Canada inviting a cab driver out to dinner.

The American who was seeking to impress the others said to his wife; "Pass the sherry, Sherry."

Shortly afterwards the Canadian said to his wife, "Pass the sweetie, Sweetie."

The cab driver thought it was cute so he did not want to be left out. He turned to his wife after she had eaten her chicken and said, "Pass the bone, dog."

Boston

A couple who was married in Washington, was on their way to New York to spend their honeymoon.

After driving for a while the man reached over to touch his wife on her legs for the first time. He quickly removed his hand when she looked at him.

She said, "Its alright now sweetheart, you can go much farther,"

The husband decided to miss the exit to New York and took her further on to Boston.

Syntax I: Dog Bone

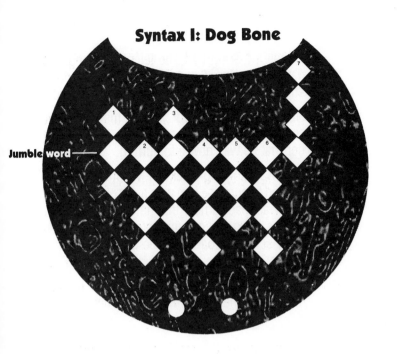

Jumble word ——

Clues

1. Denotes Negative
2. Present tense of passed
3. Good looking
4. Gone Already
5. Taxi
6. Already spoken
7. Married woman

Parts of Speech

1. _____
2. _____
3. _____
4. _____
5. _____
6. _____
7. _____

What is the jumble word

Surfing

Bring ! ! ! Bring ! ! ! The telephone rang one day. "Hello Harry" came the voice on the other end. "This is your Aunt Shiela from England."

Harry was so excited he told his aunt how successful he was at school. He indicated to her that he was now into surfing.

She was coming back on vacation, so she wanted to surprise him with a gift of some sort. She was glad to hear that he was into surfing so she bought him a complete surfing outfit; body suit, surfboard and the works.

When she reached home, she presented them to him. She couldn't believe it when he told her that he meant surfing the internet.

Which Pig

Driving down the road with her husband a woman saw a sign which read: 'Pigs For Sale". She asked him if he could turn back. He refused.

It was only after he reached home that he explained to her, he didn't want anyone to buy her.

Big Spender

My school friend came back from America. He saw that I owned a supermarket so he promised to come in and spend some money with me.

One day I saw him entering the supermarket. I thought that he was about to spend some big bucks on some items, so I asked him what he wanted.

He said a telephone call.

76

Syntax I: Surfing

Jumble word —

Clues

1. Heard during speech
2. Finish
3. Fifth Letter (alphabet)
4. Opposite of front
5. Happy
6. . . . . . . with the ears
7. Astonish

Parts of Speech

1. _____
2. _____
3. _____
4. _____
5. _____
6. _____
7. _____

Sugar

Stella, a very attractive lady in our neighbourhood went to her husband all excited one day.

She said that people always tell her that she was sweet, but she did not know that she was so sweet.

She said that she went to the doctor and he told her that she had sugar.

The husband asked her if she did not tell him (meaning the doctor) that she had thirteen children.

Foul Air

A teacher writing on the chalkboard kept passing air repeatedly.

They had an awful smell.

Every time he passed air someone would complain.

"Please teacher, someone is passing air all the time and they are dirty."

All the teacher would do is look back and say, "Would the person passing air please go outside !"

It happened about five more times and the teacher made the same appeal.

On the seventh occasion a little child got up and questioned the teacher if he could ask a favour of him.

"What favour Kevin?"

"Please teacher can you leave the classroom before you knock out somebody.

My Philosophies

It matters not who you are thought to be
but who you really are.

Life is like a mirror reflecting what you do,
if you face it smiling, it will smile right back at you.

The happiest people are those who do the most
to make others happy.

*During my schooldays the above were
passed on to me by my teachers.*

When I die don't you cry,
Don't ask yourself why.
Just put some jokes in my eulogy,
And say, "he was a man who died happy."

Answers To Quiz

1. There are no B's in the word that.
2. Four and five are nine.
3. The Arithmethical Table. $1 \times 2 = 2$
   $2 \times 2 = 4$
4.   3
       3
      33
     333
     333
     ―――
     705

5. A w.
6. Because the Hoe Hoe Hoe.
7. He took nine days.
8. Twice: once in the morning and once in a the evening.
9. She would die.
10. They used the first ball and then the new ball.

The Truth

A lady who was looking for a gift for her best friend bought this book while on holiday.

Thanks

Thanks to all persons who were of assistance to me. Your help meant more than a contribution of money.

Special thanks to Jehovah for his support and strength in guiding me through this exercise.

To Ian Moore for the layout and design, I also express my sincere thanks.